Ridgewood
Analogies

Critical and Creative Thinking across the Curriculum

BOOK TWO

George Libonate, Jr.

with
Gae Brunner • Deborah Burde
Marianne Williams • Terri Wiss

Educators Publishing Service, Inc.
Cambridge and Toronto

ACKNOWLEDGMENTS

Dr. Frederick J. Stokley, Superintendent of Schools in Ridgewood, New Jersey, initiated the idea of publishing Ridgewood curriculum. He hoped that Ridgewood could contribute to American education by sharing material that has proved particularly stimulating and effective in the Ridgewood schools.

Patricia Lane, Project Manager for Curriculum Publications, organized and supervised the team that developed the analogy material. She worked closely with the publisher as both a consultant and a facilitator.

Dennis Carroll, Art Supervisor, helped students produce quality work in a timely manner.

Joan Hartmann, Secretary, spent long hours typing, with great dedication to the project.

About the Authors, page 52

ISBN 0-8388-2290-8

April 1999 Printing

Cover art by Katie McCory

Design by Joyce Weston

1. WHAT IS AN ANALOGY?

An analogy is two sets of words that you read as if they were a sentence. The two sets of words go together in a special way. The relationship between the parts of the first set is like the relationship between the parts of the second set.

Here is an analogy:

bat : baseball : : racket : tennis ball

We read this as, *Bat* is to *baseball* as *racket* is to *tennis ball*. This means that the relationship between *bat* and *baseball* is like the relationship between *racket* and *tennis ball*. You can explain the similarity through a *relationship sentence.*

A bat is used to hit a baseball, just as a racket is used to hit a tennis ball.

In this book, you will learn to finish or solve analogies. For example,

see : eye : : hear : _____ .

We read this as, *See* is to *eye* as *hear* is to _____ .

The relationship sentence is: **You can see with your eyes, just as you can hear with your ears**.

2. WHY SHOULD YOU LEARN TO SOLVE AND CREATE ANALOGIES?

The kind of thinking you do to solve and create analogies helps you learn. It also gives you power as a problem solver. Solving and creating analogies helps learners to:

- process information for themselves
- make connections
- use information and skills to identify relationships
- improve understanding, comprehension, and long-term memory

3. HOW CAN YOU USE ANALOGIES?

You can use analogies in all of your subjects. Solving and making up your own analogies can help you understand content and develop skills.

As you use them to identify relationships and make connections, they stimulate critical and creative thinking.

Analogies can be included in all areas of study. For example, in language arts, analogies can easily be used when you work with verb tenses.

Come : came : : begin : _____

Once you recognize that *came* is the past tense of *come*, you can think about the past tense of *begin*. The missing word is *began* because that is the past tense.

In social studies, when studying the writers of important American documents, you might want to group names and documents in the following way:

Thomas Jefferson : Declaration of Independence : :
James Madison : Constitution

The relationship sentence would be, *Thomas Jefferson* was an author of the *Declaration of Independence*, just as *James Madison* was an author of the *Constitution*.

In science, you might remember the early stages of development of living creatures by writing them in analogy form:

tadpole : frog : : caterpillar : butterfly (moth)

The relationship sentence would be, A *tadpole* develops into a *frog*, just as a *caterpillar* develops into a *butterfly (moth)*.

On the next few pages you will find pre-analogy activities. These activities will help you begin to think critically.

DIRECTIONS: Choose a word from the Word Bank that is a synonym* for a word on the list.

WORD BANK

applaud	begin	carton	find
finish	illness	location	mouth
pretty	pupil	remain	repair
	vacant	warmth	

SAMPLE: end _____finish_____

Finish *is a synonym for* **end**.

---

1. empty _____

2. discover _____

3. stay _____

4. sickness _____

5. place _____

6. heat _____

7. student _____

8. start _____

9. clap _____

10. fix _____

11. beautiful _____

12. box _____

*A **synonym** is a word that means the same as another word.

DIRECTIONS: Group the words in the Word Bank under the headings *noun*, *action verb*, or *adjective*.

A *noun* is a word that names a person, place, thing, idea, or emotion: *winter*.
An *action verb* is a word that tells what is happening: *write*.
An *adjective* is a word that describes a noun: *delicious*.
Sometimes a word can be both a noun and a verb: *hunt*.

WORD BANK				
bite	cloud	complain	doctor	examine
famous	guilty	humid	hunt	invent
organ	peaceful	rough	teacher	violin

Noun	Action Verb	Adjective
1. organ	1. bite	1. famous
2.	2.	2.
3.	3.	3.
4.	4.	4.
5.	5.	5.

DIRECTIONS: Write words from the Word Bank in the appropriate sections of the Venn diagram. If the word is a noun, write it in section A. If it is a word that has three syllables, write it in section B. If it is a noun that has 3 syllables, write it in section C. A Venn diagram is a symbol made up of two or more overlapping circles. Each circle represents a group. The overlapping section shows the way some words can fit into more than one group at a time.

WORD BANK

addition	direction	easily	explorer	improving
innocent	magnet	medicine	needle	picture
powerful	president	ramp	similar	singer

SAMPLE: picture   president   innocent

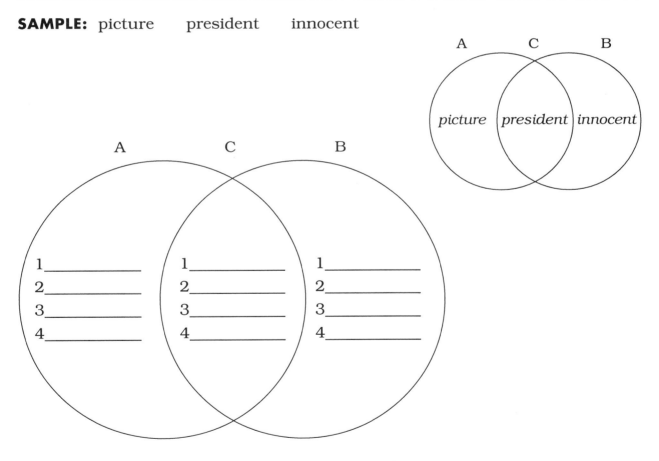

A. **Words that are nouns:** needle, singer, magnet, ramp
B. **Words that have three syllables:** easily, improving, powerful, similar
C. **Words that are nouns and have three syllables:** addition, medicine, explorer, direction

ANSWERS:

DIRECTIONS: Read the groups of words below. Number the words in each group 1, 2, and 3; going from the most general to the most specific. Use #1 for the most general idea or object.

SAMPLE: necklace   __2__
                jewelry   __1__
                locket   __3__

Jewelry is the most general word, and *locket* is the most specific.

---

1. female   _____   **7.** body of water   _____
       human   _____   ocean   _____
       woman   _____   Pacific   _____

2. elementary   _____   **8.** dessert   _____
       public school   _____   cake   _____
       school   _____   angel food   _____

3. plane   _____   **9.** wristwatch   _____
       jumbo jet   _____   timepiece   _____
       747   _____   watch   _____

4. sport   _____   **10.** subject   _____
       recreation   _____   geometry   _____
       soccer   _____   math   _____

5. teaspoon   _____   **11.** caboose   _____
       spoon   _____   train   _____
       silverware   _____   transportation _____

6. evergreen   _____   **12.** brass   _____
       tree   _____   instrument   _____
       plant   _____   trumpet   _____

DIRECTIONS: Read the sentences below. The first sentence in each group names two things. The second sentence tells one way in which they are alike.

On the line that follows, write a sentence that shows *one way in which they are different.* There may be more than one answer.

SAMPLE: A collie and a parrot are animals. They both have tails.

       POSSIBLE ANSWER:

       A collie has hair and a parrot has feathers.

---

1. A violin and a guitar are musical instruments. They both have strings.

_____

2. Carrots and peas are vegetables. They are both grown on farms.

_____

3. A hammer and a screwdriver are tools. They both have handles.

_____

4. A bench and a rocker are furniture. They are both places to sit.

_____

5. A tornado and a hurricane are storms. They both have strong winds.

_____

6. A football player and a hockey player are athletes. They both play on teams.

_____

7. A hospital and a school are buildings. They both provide service to a community.

_____

8. A bat and a mitt are pieces of sports equipment. They are both used in the game of baseball.

_____

9. Mittens and woolen scarves are clothing. They are both worn in winter.

_____

10. Popcorn and pretzels are food. They are both snacks.

_____

11. A lake and a pond are bodies of water. They are both surrounded by land.

_____

12. Whales and dolphins are mammals. They are both found in the ocean.

_____

Answers will vary. Any answer that clearly expresses contrast is acceptable.

A **descriptive analogy** shows a relationship between two sets of elements, in which one element of each set describes a characteristic, property, part, function, structure, use, position, or location of the other.

For example, in the sample "*tail* is to *dog* as *gill* is to *fish*," *tail* is one part of a *dog*, just as *gill* is one part of a *fish*.

SAMPLE:

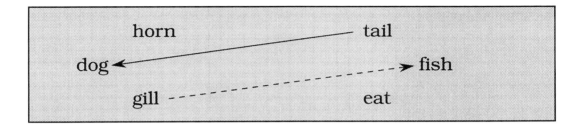

The relationship phrase is: *is one part of a*. **Tail** *is one part of a* **dog**, just as **gill** *is one part of a* **fish**.

DIRECTIONS: In the boxes below, two words that go together in a particular way are connected by an arrow. Find two other words in the box that go together in the same way.

1.

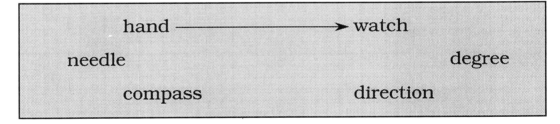

Write the relationship phrase you used to complete this analogy.

2.

Write the relationship phrase you used to complete this analogy.

3.

Write the relationship phrase you used to complete this analogy.

4.

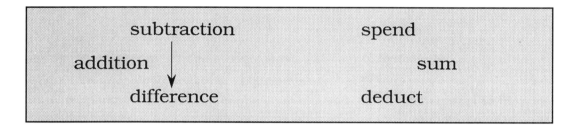

Write the relationship phrase you used to complete this analogy.

5.

Write the relationship phrase you used to complete this analogy.

6.

Write the relationship phrase you used to complete this analogy.

7.

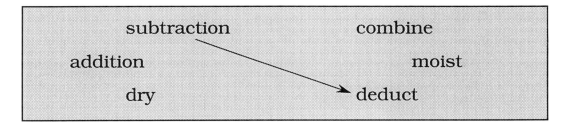

Write the relationship phrase you used to complete this analogy.

8.

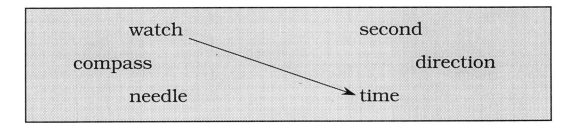

Write the relationship phrase you used to complete this analogy.

9.

Write the relationship phrase you used to complete this analogy.

10.

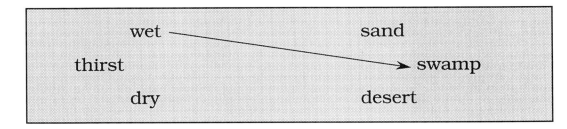

Write the relationship phrase you used to complete this analogy.

DIRECTIONS: Two words that go together in a particular way are connected by a colon. Fill in the blank with a word from the Word Bank to make another pair that goes together in the same way. Words in the Word Bank may be used more than once; some won't be used at all.

WORD BANK				
addition	arid	compass	degree	desert
empty	forest	gill	glass	music
odd	plus	product	rain	sand
song	sum	thirst	voice	water

SAMPLE: tail : dog : : **gill** : fish

The relationship is: *is one part of a.* **Tail** *is one part of a* **dog**, just as **gill** *is one part of a* **fish**.

---

1. hand : watch : : needle : _____

Write the relationship phrase you used to complete this analogy.

_____

2. even : duet : : _____ : trio

Write the relationship phrase you used to complete this analogy.

_____

3. desert : _____ : : swamp : water

Write the relationship phrase you used to complete this analogy.

_____

4. _____ : addition : : difference : subtraction

Write the relationship phrase you used to complete this analogy.

_____

5.   watch : movie : : listen : _____

Write the relationship phrase you used to complete this analogy.

_____

6.   singer : _____ : : actor : script

Write the relationship phrase you used to complete this analogy.

_____

7.   subtraction : deduct : : _____ : combine

Write the relationship phrase you used to complete this analogy.

_____

8.   _____ : direction : : watch : time

Write the relationship phrase you used to complete this analogy.

_____

9.   swamp : humid : : desert : _____

Write the relationship phrase you used to complete this analogy.

_____

10.   wet : swamp : : dry : _____

Write the relationship phrase you used to complete this analogy.

_____

DIRECTIONS: Look at the words in each incomplete analogy. Find two words in the Word Bank to combine with them to make two pairs of words that go together in the same way. Words in the Word Bank can be used more than once.

WORD BANK				
addition	compass	deduct	degree	deposit
desert	difference	direction	dry	duet
empty	even	fish	full	gill
glass	hand	hot	listen	minute
music	needle	north	odd	product
rain	singer	song	south	spend
subtraction	sum	swamp	thirst	three
time	trio	voice	water	wet

SAMPLE: tail : dog : : **gill** : **fish**

The relationship phrase is: *is one part of a.* **Tail** *is one part of a* **dog**, just as **gill** *is one part of a* **fish**.

---

1. _____ : _____ : : hand : watch

Write the relationship phrase you used to complete this analogy.

_____

2. even : _____ : : _____ : trio

Write the relationship phrase you used to complete this analogy.

_____

3. _____ : sand : : swamp : _____

Write the relationship phrase you used to complete this analogy.

_____

4. _____ : addition : : _____ : subtraction

Write the relationship phrase you used to complete this analogy.

_____

5. watch : movie : : _____ : _____

Write the relationship phrase you used to complete this analogy.

_____

6. _____ : _____ : : actor : script

Write the relationship phrase you used to complete this analogy.

_____

7. subtraction : _____ : : _____ : combine

Write the relationship phrase you used to complete this analogy.

_____

8. _____ : direction : : watch : _____

Write the relationship phrase you used to complete this analogy.

_____

9. _____ : humid : : _____ : arid

Write the relationship phrase you used to complete this analogy.

_____

10. wet : swamp : : _____ : : _____

Write the relationship phrase you used to complete this analogy.

_____

DIRECTIONS: Here is a real challenge: Create your own analogies to go with a given relationship phrase or create both the analogy and the relationship phrase. Use the Word Bank below. There may be more than one correct answer. Remember: the relationship phrase must be the same for each pair.

WORD BANK				
arm	body	compass	degree	deposit
desert	difference	direction	dry	duet
empty	even	fish	full	glass
hand	hot	house	minute	music
needle	north	odd	product	roof
sand	second	south	spend	subtraction
sum	swamp	thirst	three	time
trio	voice	watch	water	wet

SAMPLE: Create an analogy using this relationship phrase: *is one part of a(n)*

arm : _____ : : _____ : _____

The answer to the first part could be **body**, since **arm** *is one part of a* body. The analogy in the second part would be any pair of words in the Word Bank that also fits the relationship phrase.

arm : body : : roof : house

Another analogy could be:

arm : body : : second : minute

1. Create an analogy using this relationship: *is a moving part of a.*

_____ : _____ : : needle : _____

DIRECTIONS: Create this analogy by finding a word in the Word Bank that forms a relationship with the given word. Then find two other words that go together in exactly the same way.

2. wet : _____ : : _____ : _____

Write the relationship phrase that was used.

Relationship phrase: _____

DIRECTIONS: Now try creating some analogies from scratch, using the words in the Word Bank.

3. Write a relationship phrase and create an analogy.

Relationship phrase: _____

_____ : _____ : : _____ : _____

4. Write a relationship phrase and create an analogy.

Relationship phrase: _____

_____ : _____ : : _____ : _____

A **comparative analogy** shows a relationship between two sets of elements in which one or more qualities are the same and one or more are different.

   For example, in the sample "*Large* is to *big* as *small* is to *little*," *large* and *big* are synonyms. They have the same meaning but are spelled differently; *small* and *little* also are synonyms.

SAMPLE:

The relationship phrase is: *is a synonym for*. **End** *is a synonym for* **finish**, just as **small** *is a synonym for* **little**.

DIRECTIONS: A line connects two words that go together in a special way. Find two other words in the frame that go together in the same way.

1.

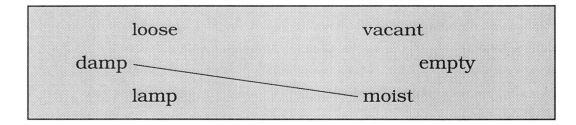

Write the relationship phrase you used to complete this analogy.

_____

2.

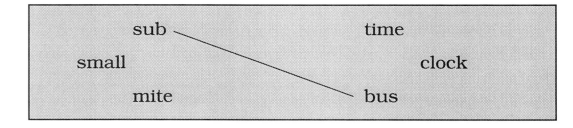

Write the relationship phrase you used to complete this analogy.

_____

3.

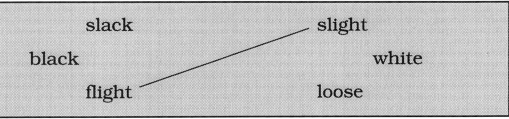

slack   slight

black   white

flight   loose

Write the relationship phrase you used to complete this analogy.

4.

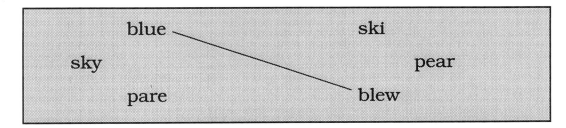

blue   ski

sky   pear

pare   blew

Write the relationship phrase you used to complete this analogy.

5.

wolf   liar

lair   rail

water   flow

Write the relationship phrase you used to complete this analogy.

6.

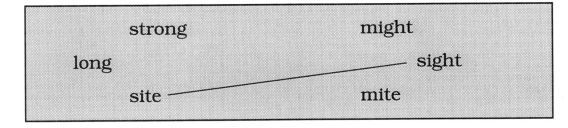

strong   might

long   sight

site   mite

Write the relationship phrase you used to complete this analogy.

7.

full   meat

empty   earn

team   near

Write the relationship phrase you used to complete this analogy.

8.

magnet   combine

needle   join

entice   attract

Write the relationship phrase you used to complete this analogy.

9.

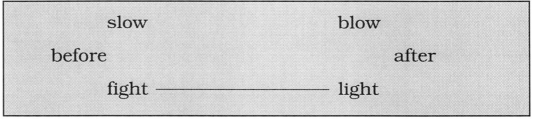

slow   blow

before   after

fight ——————— light

Write the relationship phrase you used to complete this analogy.

10.

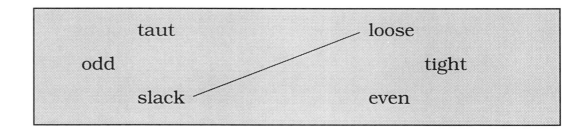

taut   loose

odd   tight

slack   even

Write the relationship phrase you used to complete this analogy.

DIRECTIONS: The two words that are connected by a colon go together in a special way. Fill in the blank with a word from the Word Bank to make another pair that goes together in the same way. Words in the Word Bank may be used more than once.

WORD BANK				
black	blew	blow	blue	deduct
earn	empty	entice	first	flow
full	meat	might	mite	pare
	tight	small	vacant	

SAMPLE: end : finish : : little : **small**

The relationship phrase is: *is a synonym for.*
End *is a synonym for* **finish**, just as **small** *is a synonym for* **little**.

---

1. damp : moist : : vacant : _____

Write the relationship phrase you used to complete this analogy.

---

2. sub : bus : : time : _____

Write the relationship phrase you used to complete this analogy.

---

3. fight : slight : : _____ : slack

Write the relationship phrase you used to complete this analogy.

---

4. _____ : pear : : blew : blue

Write the relationship phrase you used to complete this analogy.

_____

5. wolf : _____ : : liar : rail

Write the relationship phrase you used to complete this analogy.

_____

6. site : sight : : mite : _____

Write the relationship phrase you used to complete this analogy.

_____

7. _____ : team : : near : earn

Write the relationship phrase you used to complete this analogy.

_____

8. combine : join : : attract : _____

Write the relationship phrase you used to complete this analogy.

_____

9. _____ : slow : : fight : light

Write the relationship phrase you used to complete this analogy.

_____

10. loose : slack : : taut : _____

Write the relationship phrase you used to complete this analogy.

_____

DIRECTIONS: Look at the words in each incomplete analogy. Choose two words from the Word Bank that make two pairs of words that go together in the same way. Words in the Word Bank can be used more than once.

WORD BANK				
attract	black	blew	blow	blue
car	damp	earn	empty	entice
first	flew	flow	join	liar
light	loose	meat	might	mite
moist	pare	plus	rain	repel
repulse	sight	slack	slight	small
taut	time	small	vacant	wolf

SAMPLE: end : finish : : **little** : **small**

The relationship phrase is: *is a synonym for.*
Finish *is a synonym for* **end**, just as **small** *is a synonym for* **little**.

---

1. vacant : _____ : : damp : _____

Write the relationship phrase you used to complete this analogy.

_____

2. sub : bus : : _____ : _____

Write the relationship phrase you used to complete this analogy.

_____

3. flight : _____ : : _____ : slack

Write the relationship phrase you used to complete this analogy.

_____

4. _____ : pear : : blew : _____

Write the relationship phrase you used to complete this analogy.

_____

5. wolf : _____ : : _____ : rail

Write the relationship phrase you used to complete this analogy.

_____

6. site : _____ : : mite : _____

Write the relationship phrase you used to complete this analogy.

_____

7. _____ : team : : near : _____

Write the relationship phrase you used to complete this analogy.

_____

8. combine : _____ : : attract : _____

Write the relationship phrase you used to complete this analogy.

_____

9. _____ : slow : : fight : _____

Write the relationship phrase you used to complete this analogy.

_____

10. _____ : slack : : _____ : tight

Write the relationship phrase you used to complete this analogy.

_____

DIRECTIONS: Here is a real challenge: Create your own analogies to go with a given relationship phrase or create both the analogy and the relationship phrase. Use the Word Bank below. There may be more than one correct answer. Remember: the relationship phrase must be the same for each pair.

SAMPLE: Create an analogy using this relationship : *is a homophone for*

might : _____ : : _____ : _____

The answer to the first part could be **mite**, since **might** *is a homophone for* **mite**. The analogy in the second part would be any pair of words in the Word Bank that also fits the relationship phrase.

might : mite : : blew : blue

Another analogy could be:

might : mite : : rain : rein

Rain *is a homophone for* **rein**, just as **might** *is a homophone for* **mite**.

WORD BANK			
attract	black	blew	blow
blue	car	damp	earn
empty	entice	first	flew
flow	join	lair	light
loose	marine	meat	meet
might	mite	moist	pair
pare	rain	rein	remain
repel	repulse	sight	sky
slack	slight	taught	taut
time	vacant	visual	wolf

1. Create an analogy using this relationship: *is a synonym for.*

_____ : _____ : : vacant : _____

DIRECTIONS: Create this analogy by finding a word in the Word Bank that forms a relationship with the given word. Then find two other words that go together in exactly the same way.

2. blew : _____ : : _____ : _____

Write the relationship phrase that was used.

Relationship phrase: _____

DIRECTIONS: Now try creating some analogies from scratch, using the words in the Word Bank.

3. Write a relationship phrase and create an analogy.

Relationship phrase: _____

_____ : _____ : : _____ : _____

4. Write a relationship phrase and create an analogy.

Relationship phrase: _____

_____ : _____ : : _____ : _____

A **categorical** analogy shows a relationship between two sets of elements, in which one element of each set is a member of the other's category.

For example, in the sample "*milk is to liquid as fir is to tree*," *milk* is a member of the *liquid* category, just as *fir* is a member of the *tree* category.

SAMPLE:

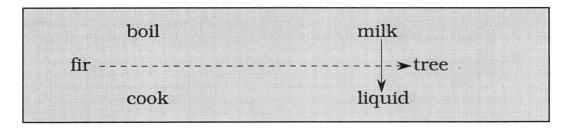

The relationship phrase is: *is an example of.*
Milk *is an example of* **liquid**, just as **fir** *is an example of* **tree**.

DIRECTIONS: An arrow connects two words that go together in a special way. Find two other words in the frame that go together in the same way.

1.

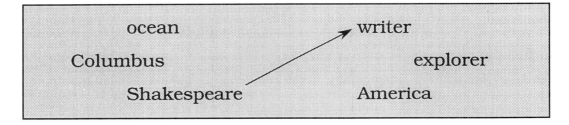

Write the relationship phrase you used to complete this analogy.

2.

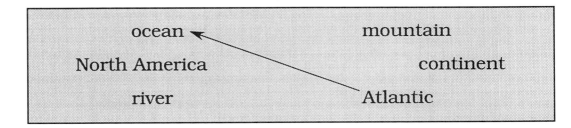

Write the relationship phrase you used to complete this analogy.

3.

Write the relationship phrase you used to complete this analogy.

4.

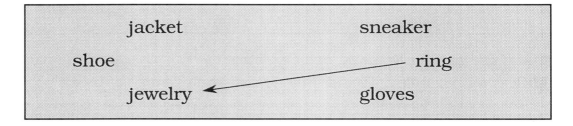

Write the relationship phrase you used to complete this analogy.

5.

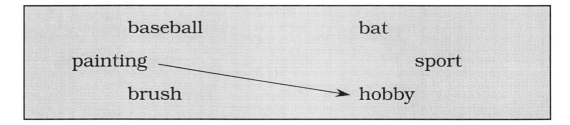

Write the relationship phrase you used to complete this analogy.

6.

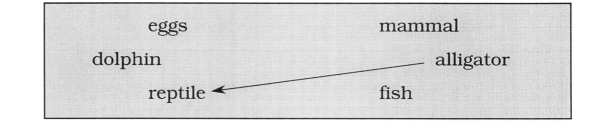

Write the relationship phrase you used to complete this analogy.

7.

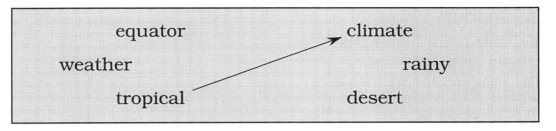

equator   climate

weather   rainy

tropical   desert

Write the relationship phrase you used to complete this analogy.

8.

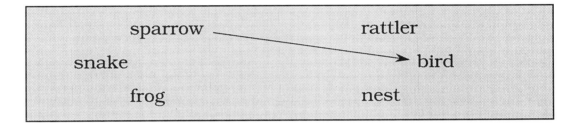

sparrow   rattler

snake   bird

frog   nest

Write the relationship phrase you used to complete this analogy.

9.

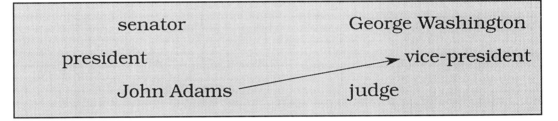

senator   George Washington

president   vice-president

John Adams   judge

Write the relationship phrase you used to complete this analogy.

10.

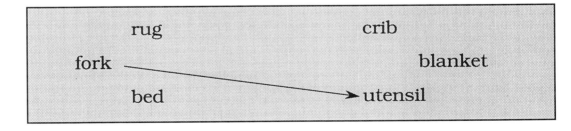

rug   crib

fork   blanket

bed   utensil

Write the relationship phrase you used to complete this analogy.

DIRECTIONS: Two words that go together in a special way are connected by a colon. Find two other words in the Word Bank that go together in the same way. Words in the Word Bank may be used more than once.

WORD BANK			
bat	bed	brush	chair
continent	den	desert	eggs
explorer	fiction	food	gloves
jacket	judge	mammal	ocean
president	rainy	rattler	rug
sneaker	sport	tree	writer

SAMPLE: milk : liquid : : fir : **tree**

The relationship phrase is: *is an example of.*
Milk *is an example of* **liquid**, just as **fir** *is an example of* **tree**.

---

1. Columbus : _____ : : Shakespeare : writer

Write the relationship phrase you used to complete this analogy.

_____

2. North America : _____ : : Atlantic : ocean

Write the relationship phrase you used to complete this analogy.

_____

3. lion : cat : : _____ : writing

Write the relationship phrase you used to complete this analogy.

_____

4. _____ : shoe : : ring : jewelry

Write the relationship phrase you used to complete this analogy.

---

5. painting : hobby : : baseball : _____

Write the relationship phrase you used to complete this analogy.

---

6. dolphin : _____ : : alligator : reptile

Write the relationship phrase you used to complete this analogy.

---

7. tropical : climate : : _____ : weather

Write the relationship phrase you used to complete this analogy.

---

8. _____ : snake : : sparrow : bird

Write the relationship phrase you used to complete this analogy.

---

9. John Adams : vice-president : : George Washington : _____

Write the relationship phrase you used to complete this analogy.

---

10. crib : _____ : : fork : utensil

Write the relationship phrase you used to complete this analogy.

DIRECTIONS: Look at the words in each incomplete analogy. Find two words in the Word Bank to make the pairs of words go together in the same way. Words in the Word Bank can be used more than once.

WORD BANK			
baseball	bat	bed	bird
brush	cat	chair	climate
continent	crib	den	desert
dolphin	equator	explorer	fiction
fir	food	George Washington	gulf
jacket	jewelry	judge	mammal
meat	North America	president	rainy
rattler	rocker	Shakespeare	sneaker
sport	tiger	tree	writer

SAMPLE: milk : liquid : : **fir** : **tree**

The relationship phrase is: *is an example of.*
Milk *is an example of* **liquid**, just as **fir** *is an example of* **tree**.

---

1. Columbus : _____ : : Shakespeare : _____

Write the relationship phrase you used to complete this analogy.

_____

2. _____ : _____ : : Atlantic : ocean

Write the relationship phrase you used to complete this analogy.

_____

3. lion : _____ : : _____ : writing

Write the relationship phrase you used to complete this analogy.

_____

4. _____ : shoe: : ring : _____

Write the relationship phrase you used to complete this analogy.

_____

5. painting : hobby : : _____ : _____

Write the relationship phrase you used to complete this analogy.

_____

6. _____ : _____ : : alligator : reptile

Write the relationship phrase you used to complete this analogy.

_____

7. tropical : _____ : : _____ : weather

Write the relationship phrase you used to complete this analogy.

_____

8. _____ : snake : : sparrow : _____

Write the relationship phrase you used to complete this analogy.

_____

9. John Adams : vice-president : : _____ : _____

Write the relationship phrase you used to complete this analogy.

_____

10. _____ : _____ : : fork : utensil

Write the relationship phrase you used to complete this analogy.

_____

DIRECTIONS: Here is a real challenge: Create your own analogies to go with a given relationship phrase or create both the analogy and the relationship phrase. Use the Word Bank below. There may be more than one correct answer. Remember: the relationship phrase must be the same for each pair.

SAMPLE: Create an analogy using this relationship phrase: *is one kind of.*

dolphin : _____ : : _____ : _____

The answer to the first part would be **mammal**, since dolphin *is one kind of* mammal. The analogy in the second part would be any pair of words in the Word Bank that fits the relationship phrase.

dolphin : mammal : : rattler : snake

Another analogy could be:

dolphin : mammal : : meat : food

WORD BANK			
baseball	bat	bed	bird
book	building	cat	chair
checkers	climate	clothing	continent
crib	day	den	desert
dolphin	earring	explorer	fiction
food	game	George Washington	gloves
jacket	jewelry	judge	library
mammal	meat	North America	president
rainy	rattler	rocker	Shakespeare
shirt	snake	sneaker	sport
	tiger	writer	

1. Create an analogy using this relationship: *is an example of a.*

_____ : _____ : : rocker : _____

DIRECTIONS: Create this analogy by finding a word in the Word Bank that forms a relationship with the given word. Then find two other words that go together in exactly the same way.

2. tiger : _____ : : _____ : _____

Write the relationship phrase that was used.

Relationship phrase: _____

DIRECTIONS: Now create some analogies.

3. Write a relationship phrase and create an analogy.

Relationship phrase: _____

_____ : _____ : : _____ : _____

4. Write a relationship phrase and create an analogy.

Relationship phrase: _____

_____ : _____ : : _____ : _____

A **serial** analogy shows a relationship between two sets of elements, in which one element of each set follows the other in serial order by time, size, process, or quantity. The series may also indicate degree of difference, intensity, or importance.

For example, in the sample "*fifth* is to *sixth* as *Halloween* is to *Thanksgiving*," the first member of each set comes before the other in time.

SAMPLE:

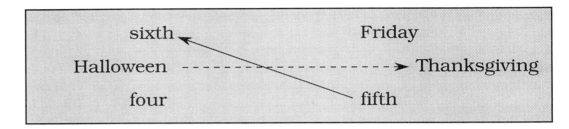

The relationship phrase is: *comes before*.
Fifth *comes before* **sixth**, just as **Halloween** *comes before* **Thanksgiving**.

DIRECTIONS: An arrow connects two words that go together in a special way. Find two other words in the frame that go together in the same way.

1.

Write the relationship phrase you used to complete this analogy.

2.

Write the relationship phrase you used to complete this analogy.

3.

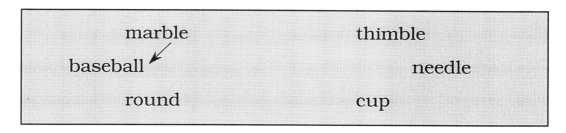

Write the relationship phrase you used to complete this analogy.

4.

Write the relationship phrase you used to complete this analogy.

5.

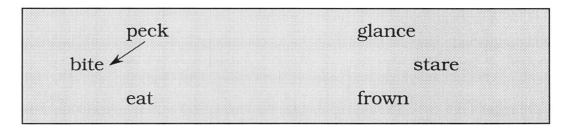

Write the relationship phrase you used to complete this analogy.

6.

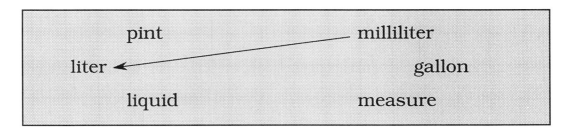

Write the relationship phrase you used to complete this analogy.

7.

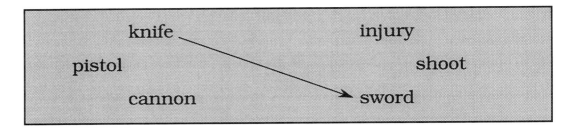

Write the relationship phrase you used to complete this analogy.

8.

Write the relationship phrase you used to complete this analogy.

9.

Write the relationship phrase you used to complete this analogy.

10.

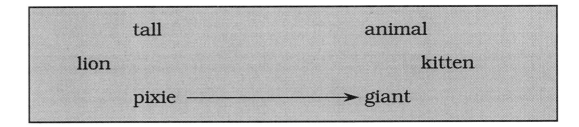

Write the relationship phrase you used to complete this analogy.

DIRECTIONS: A colon connects two words that go together in a special way. Fill in the blank with a word from the Word Bank to make another pair that goes together in the same way. Words in the Word Bank may be used more than once.

WORD BANK

animal	boil	cannon	eat
frigid	frown	gash	kitten
hill	liquid	measure	midnight
needle	pint	puddle	rain
scissors	secret	stare	Thanksgiving
thimble	time	water	whisper

SAMPLE: fifth : sixth : : Halloween : **Thanksgiving**

The relationship phrase is: *comes before.*
Fifth *comes before* **sixth**, just as **Halloween** *comes before* **Thanksgiving**.

---

1. dawn : noon : : dusk : _____

Write the relationship phrase you used to complete this analogy.

---

2. nick : _____ : : tear : shred

Write the relationship phrase you used to complete this analogy.

---

3. _____ : cup : : marble : baseball

Write the relationship phrase you used to complete this analogy.

---

4. hill : mountain : : _____ : lake

Write the relationship phrase you used to complete this analogy.

_____

5. glance : _____ : : peck : bite

Write the relationship phrase you used to complete this analogy.

_____

6. _____ : gallon : : milliliter : liter

Write the relationship phrase you used to complete this analogy.

_____

7. pistol : _____ : : knife : sword

Write the relationship phrase you used to complete this analogy.

_____

8. lukewarm : hot : : cool : _____

Write the relationship phrase you used to complete this analogy.

_____

9. surprise : shock : : _____ : shout

Write the relationship phrase you used to complete this analogy.

_____

10. pixie : giant : : _____ : lion

Write the relationship phrase you used to complete this analogy.

_____

DIRECTIONS: Look at the words that are given in each incomplete analogy. Find and combine two words from the Word Bank to make the two pairs of words go together in the same way. Words in the Word Bank can be used more than once.

WORD BANK

animal	cannon	cool	cup	dusk
frown	gallon	gash	giant	glance
Halloween	hot	injury	lake	lion
liquid	marble	midnight	needle	nick
pint	shout	puddle	secret	stare
surprise	sword	Thanksgiving	time	whisper

SAMPLE: fifth : sixth : : **Halloween** : **Thanksgiving**

The relationship phrase is: *comes before.*
Fifth *comes before* **sixth**, just as **Halloween** *comes before* **Thanksgiving**.

---

1.   dawn : noon : : _____ : _____

Write the relationship phrase you used to complete this analogy.

---

2.   _____ : _____ : : tear : shred

Write the relationship phrase you used to complete this analogy.

---

3.   thimble : _____ : : _____ : baseball

Write the relationship phrase you used to complete this analogy.

---

4. hill : mountain : : _____ : _____

Write the relationship phrase you used to complete this analogy.

_____

5. _____ : _____ : : peck : bite

Write the relationship phrase you used to complete this analogy.

_____

6. _____ : _____ : : milliliter : liter

Write the relationship phrase you used to complete this analogy.

_____

7. pistol : _____ : : knife : _____

Write the relationship phrase you used to complete this analogy.

_____

8. lukewarm : _____ : : _____ : frigid

Write the relationship phrase you used to complete this analogy.

_____

9. _____ : shock : : _____ : shout

Write the relationship phrase you used to complete this analogy.

_____

10. pixie : _____ : : kitten : _____

Write the relationship phrase you used to complete this analogy.

_____

DIRECTIONS: Here is a real challenge: Create your own analogies to go with a given relationship phrase or create both the analogy and the relationship phrase. Use the Word Bank below. There may be more than one correct answer. Remember: the relationship phrase must be the same for each pair.

SAMPLE: Create an analogy using this relationship phrase: *is less than a*

       cup : _____ : : _____ : _____

The answer to the first part would be **pint**, since cup *is less than a* **pint**. The analogy in the second part could be any pair of words in the Word Bank that fits the relationship phrase.

       cup : pint : : quart : gallon

Cup *is less than a* **pint**.

Another analogy could be:

       cup : quart : : drop : puddle

Drop *is less than a* **puddle**.

WORD BANK			
animal	boil	breakfast	butterfly
cannon	caterpillar	cool	cup
desert	drop	dusk	five
frown	gallon	gash	glance
gun	hot	knife	lake
lion	liquid	lunch	marble
midnight	needle	nick	pint
shout	puddle	quart	rain
salad	secret	stare	study
surprise	sword	ten	test
	time	whisper	

1. Create an analogy using this relationship phrase: *comes before*

   _____ : _____ : : breakfast : _____

DIRECTIONS: Create this analogy by finding a word in the Word Bank that forms a relationship with the given word. Then find two other words that go together in exactly the same way.

2. gun : _____ : : _____ : _____
Write the relationship phrase you used.

Relationship phrase: _____

DIRECTIONS: Now create your own analogies.

3. Write a relationship phrase and create an analogy.

Relationship phrase: _____

   _____ : _____ : : _____ : _____

4. Write a relationship phrase and create an analogy.

Relationship phrase: _____

   _____ : _____ : : _____ : _____

A **causal** analogy shows a relationship between two sets of elements, in which one element of each set changes or affects the other element. The change may involve reversal, reflection, a mathematical operation, or change in form, tense, or part of speech.

For example, in the sample "*tip* is to *pit* as *pan* is to *nap*," the first member of each was *reversed* to form the second member.

SAMPLE:

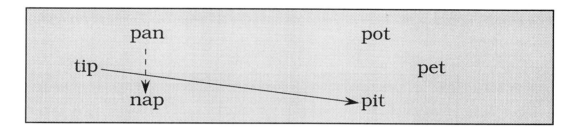

The relationship phrase is: *is the reverse of.*
Tip *is the reverse of* **pit**, just as **pan** *is the reverse of* **nap**.

DIRECTIONS:

A line connects two words that go together in a special way. Find two other words in the frame that go together in the same way.

1.

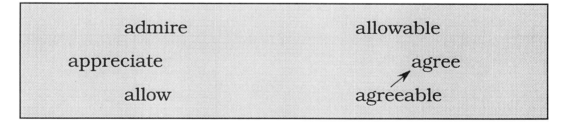

Write the relationship phrase you used to complete this analogy.

2.

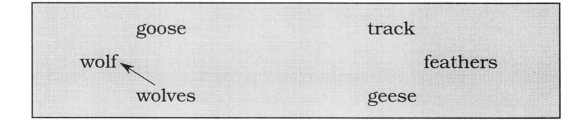

Write the relationship phrase you used to complete this analogy.

3.

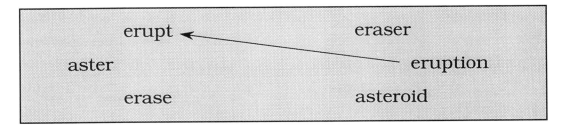

Write the relationship phrase you used to complete this analogy.

4.

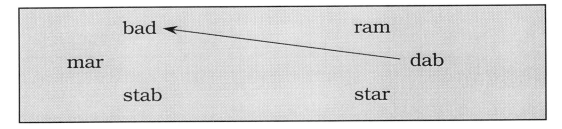

Write the relationship phrase you used to complete this analogy.

5.

Write the relationship phrase you used to complete this analogy.

6.

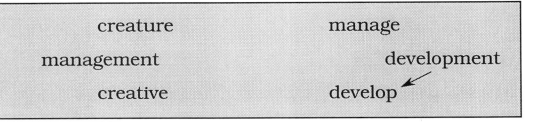

Write the relationship phrase you used to complete this analogy.

7.

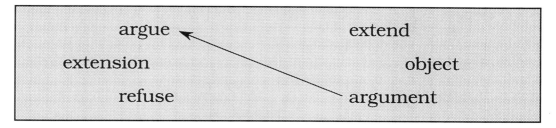

Write the relationship phrase you used to complete this analogy.

8.

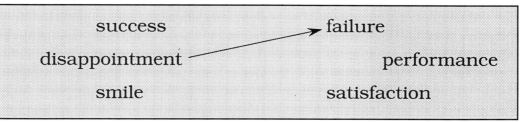

Write the relationship phrase you used to complete this analogy.

9.

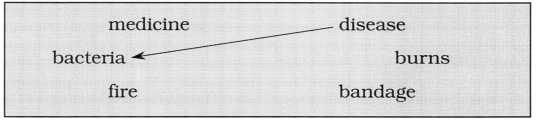

Write the relationship phrase you used to complete this analogy.

10.

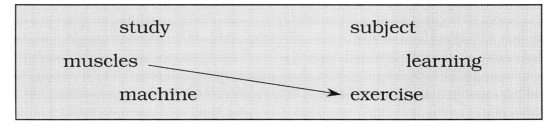

Write the relationship phrase you used to complete this analogy.

DIRECTIONS: Two words that go together in a special way are connected by a colon. Fill in the blank with a word from the Word Bank to make another pair that goes together in the same way. Words in the Word Bank may be used more than once.

WORD BANK			
accurate	admire	allow	bandage
disagreement	emit	eraser	extension
feathers	fire	germs	goose
hair	learning	light	lightly
management	mar	nap	pencil
performance	smile	success	textbook

SAMPLE: tip : pit : : pan : **nap**

The relationship phrase is: *is the reverse of.*
Tip *is the reverse of* **pit**, just as **pan** *is the reverse of* **nap**.

---

1. agreeable : agree : : allowable : _____

Write the relationship phrase you used to complete this analogy.

_____

2. wolves : wolf : : geese : _____

Write the relationship phrase you used to complete this analogy.

_____

3. _____ : erase : : eruption : erupt

Write the relationship phrase you used to complete this analogy.

_____

4. _____ : ram : : dab : bad

Write the relationship phrase you used to complete this analogy.

_____

5. flow : wolf : : _____ : time

Write the relationship phrase you used to complete this analogy.

_____

6. _____ : manage : : development : develop

Write the relationship phrase you used to complete this analogy.

_____

7. argument : argue : : _____ : extend

Write the relationship phrase you used to complete this analogy.

_____

8. satisfaction : _____ : : disappointment : failure

Write the relationship phrase you used to complete this analogy.

_____

9. disease : bacteria : : burns : _____

Write the relationship phrase you used to complete this analogy.

_____

10. muscle : exercise: : _____ : study

Write the relationship phrase you used to complete this analogy.

_____

DIRECTIONS: Look at the words in each incomplete analogy. Find two words in the Word Bank to combine with them to make two pairs of words that go together in the same way. Words in the Word Bank can be used more than once.

WORD BANK			
allow	allowable	bacteria	disappointment
discourage	emit	eraser	eruption
exercise	extend	extension	failure
fire	geese	goose	learning
light	machine	manage	management
mar	medicine	moose	nap
pan	pencil	performance	ram
smile	strong	subject	success
textbook	volcano	wolf	wolves

SAMPLE: tip : pit : : **pan** : **nap**

The relationship phrase is: *is the reverse of.*
Tip *is the reverse of* **pit**, just as **pan** *is the reverse of* **nap**.

---

1. agreeable : agree : : _____ : _____

Write the relationship phrase you used to complete this analogy.

_____

2. _____ : _____ : : wolves : wolf

Write the relationship phrase you used to complete this analogy.

_____

3. _____ : erase : : _____ : erupt

Write the relationship phrase you used to complete this analogy.

_____

4. _____ : _____ : : dab : bad

Write the relationship phrase you used to complete this analogy.

_____

5. flow : _____ : : _____ : time

Write the relationship phrase you used to complete this analogy.

_____

6. _____ : _____ : : development : develop

Write the relationship phrase you used to complete this analogy.

_____

7. argument : argue : : _____ : _____

Write the relationship phrase you used to complete this analogy.

_____

8. satisfaction : _____ : : disappointment : _____

Write the relationship phrase you used to complete this analogy.

_____

9. disease : _____ : : burns : _____

Write the relationship phrase you used to complete this analogy.

_____

10. muscle : _____ : : _____ : study

Write the relationship phrase you used to complete this analogy.

_____

DIRECTIONS: Here is a real challenge: Create your own analogies to go with a given relationship phrase or create both the analogy and the relationship phrase. Use the Word Bank below. There may be more than one correct answer. Remember: the relationship phrase must be the same for each pair.

SAMPLE: Create an analogy using this relationship phrase: *is the plural of.*

wolves: _____ : : _____ : _____

The answer to the first part would be **wolf**, since wolves *is the plural of* **wolf**. The analogy in the second part would be any pair of plural and singular words found in the Word Bank.

wolves : wolf : : volcanoes : volcano

Volcanoes *is the plural of* **volcano**, just as **wolves** *is the plural of* **wolf**.

Another analogy could be:

wolves : wolf : : lights : light

Lights *is the plural of* **light**, just as **wolves** *is the plural of* **wolf**.

WORD BANK			
allow	allowable	anger	bacteria
disagree	disappointment	discourage	disease
emit	erase	eraser	exercise
extend	extension	failure	fire
flow	frown	geese	goose
happiness	heat	improvement	learning
light	lights	manage	management
mar	medicine	moose	perform
performance	practice	ram	sick
sickness	smile	spark	subject
success	volcano	volcanoes	wolf
	wolves		

1. Create an analogy using this relationship phrase:

_____ is the reverse of _____

_____ : _____ : : mar : _____

DIRECTIONS: Create this analogy by finding a word in the Word Bank that forms a relationship with the given word. Then find two other words that go together in exactly the same way.

2. disease : _____ : : _____ : _____

Write the relationship phrase that was used.

Relationship phrase: _____

DIRECTIONS: Now create your own analogies.

3. Write a relationship phrase and create an analogy.

Relationship phrase: _____

_____ : _____ : : _____ : _____

4. Write a relationship phrase and create an analogy.

Relationship phrase: _____

_____ : _____ : : _____ : _____

ABOUT THE AUTHORS

George Libonate, Jr., the architect of Ridgewood's analogies program, has been an educator for thirty-one years. With a masters degree from Teachers College, Columbia University, and a Ph.D. from Rutgers University, he has taught at the elementary, secondary, and college levels, and has been a principal in Ridgewood for the last four years. His particular interest is helping teachers engage students in critical thinking and problem solving. He created groundbreaking workshops for teachers to develop the four types of thinking: verbal reasoning, sequences, analogies, and memory. These workshops were the seeds of the analogies program that is now used throughout the Ridgewood elementary schools.

Gae Brunner, a teacher for twenty-four years, teaches fourth and fifth grade in Ridgewood. She has a masters degree in reading and has been a reading specialist and resource room teacher. She is an author of the district social studies test which emphasizes analogies related to content.

Deborah Burde, who has a masters degree in science and teaching, teaches third grade, and was in charge of developing critical thinking units at one of Ridgewood's elementary schools.

Marianne Williams teaches fifth grade. A teacher for twenty-three years, she has a masters degree in administration and supervision, and developed the in-service program for the district. She worked on the district social studies and science tests that evaluate concept development in the subject areas through analogies, verbal reasoning, sequences, and memory.

Terri Wiss, a teacher for twenty-eight years, teaches a multi-age 4-5 class. She has a masters degree in learning disabilities and began her teaching career teaching emotionally disturbed teenagers.